THE BATTLE OF
EGYPT

Sherman Tank Driver

The Army   *at War*

CONTENTS

PREPARED FOR THE WAR OFFICE
BY THE
MINISTRY OF INFORMATION.

CROWN COPYRIGHT RESERVED.

FIRST PUBLISHED 1943.

To be purchased from His Majesty's Stationery
Office at York House, Kingsway London,
W.C.2 ; 120, George Street, Edinburgh, 2 ;
39/41, King Street, Manchester, 2 ; 1, St.
Andrew's Crescent, Cardiff ; 80, Chichester
Street, Belfast ; or through any bookseller.
Printed by Odhams (Watford) Ltd., Watford.

Price 7*d.* or 40 copies for 20*s.* net.

S.O. Code No. 70—415*.

*In " Destruction of an Army " (H.M.S.O., 7d.
with 58 pictures and 3 maps) you may read an
account of the earlier desert fighting.*

*There are many men and women in the
Forces who would welcome a chance of
reading this book. If you hand it in to the
nearest Post Office, it will go to them.*

The Approach to the Battle

EVERY PICTURE in this book tells a story ; and together the pictures tell the story of how the pendulum which had been swinging to and fro on the south-east shores of the Mediterranean for two years came to rest with a most satisfying click hard over in our favour. The book shows and briefly describes the battle up to the complete clearance of the enemy from Egyptian soil, for the Battle of Egypt is an episode in itself.

An earlier book—*Destruction of an Army*—told how, between December, 1940 and February, 1941, General Wavell swept the Italians out of Cyrenaica. Having reached the Gulf of Sirte, the General and the British Government had to decide whether to pursue the offensive in the hope of clearing everything up to French North Africa, or to send substantial help to the Greeks. Both agreed that the Greeks must come first, and a substantial part of General Wavell's army was therefore shipped across to Greece. In consequence, our positions in North Africa were very thinly held ; and before reinforcements could arrive from home or from East Africa, the Germans, who had been forced to come to the rescue of the Italians, attacked with two armoured divisions and swept our men back to the Egyptian frontier. This was held, and so was Tobruk, the defence and supply of which was an eight months' epic. Tobruk was a thorn deep in the enemy's flank ; and its possession governed the strategy of the offensive launched on November 18th, 1941, by General Wavell's successor, General Auchinleck.

Once more, after hard fighting, the pursuit swept across Cyrenaica to El Agheila, on the eastern angle of the Gulf of Sirte. This story is told fully in another book— *They Sought out Rommel*—the diary of one of the Public Relations Officers who was in the thick of the battle. Though an unquestionable victory, our attack neither crippled nor disorganised the enemy enough to prevent him standing on the strong position at El Agheila. The forces which we could supply at that time in this region were too weak for attack and too strong for a mere screen. Rommel's counter-attack drove us back as far as the line Gazala-Bir Hacheim, and restored to him the use of a number of essential supply ports, notably Benghazi. There, for four months, the two armies glared at each other, both working like beavers to make themselves strong enough to attack and too strong to be attacked. Thanks to his shorter supply lines from Greece and Italy, the enemy was ready first. On June 2nd, 1942, he attacked with his full strength, established a gap in our minefields about half-way down the line, held on to the gap resolutely, and started to enlarge it. For eleven days, the southern bastion of Bir Hacheim, manned by a French garrison, held out against the fiercest attacks, and prevented the enemy from exploiting the gap. So long as it held, the battle generally seemed to be going well ; but when it was evacuated under orders, deterioration was rapid. Between June 11th and 13th, tank battles resulted in disproportionate losses to our armour, and the whole army was involved in retreat.

It had been hoped to hold Tobruk once again and counter-attack from the Egyptian frontier. But this time Tobruk succumbed to a powerful attack within thirty-six hours. General Auchinleck had lost both the lever for a counter-offensive and about 23,000 men made prisoner. The blow was very nearly mortal. The remains of the Eighth Army had to retreat rapidly over the frontier, back past Sidi Barrani, past Mersa Matruh and back a hundred miles more to El Alamein, where there is a gap of only forty miles between the sea and the generally impassable salty marsh of the Qattara Depression. At El Alamein General Auchinleck, who had himself taken over the tactical direction of the battle, called for a stand.

It was both the last and the best defensive position from which to deny Alexandria and the Nile Delta—only sixty miles away—to the enemy. To the north, the coastal road and railway run over level sandy desert, not far from the salt lagoons which fringe the sea. In the centre are ridges and hillocks on which a

film of sand covers underlying rock. In the south, the rock breaks through the sand into outcrops, and then falls away in a sheer cliff to the Qattara Depression. South of the depression again stretch soft sand-hills impassable for cars, and the single track from Siwa to the Bahariya oasis and the Nile Valley can be held with ease against an invader. The El Alamein-Qattara position cannot therefore be turned. It can only be pierced by a frontal attack, and that is what Rommel set himself to do.

On June 30th, he launched against it the tanks of the Littorio Division, but they were driven back with heavy loss by the remains of our armour. Next day, his infantry had come up, and he flung them straight at the South African Division holding the north end of the position. Every attack was bloodily repulsed. Further south, the battle-worn 4th Indian Division dealt faithfully with the tanks all day. But when the assault was renewed at night, an Indian strong-point was over-run. Rommel thought he was through; and on July 2nd the German High Command announced to the world that he was " pursuing the beaten British into the Nile Valley."

But this critical day in fact witnessed his frustration. When he tried to " pursue " he was furiously counter-attacked, and by night-fall had started to withdraw. Renewed attacks on the next two days proved equally futile and costly. Thereafter the 9th Australian Division counter-attacked and took Tell El Eisa hill. For some days longer the battle swayed bloodily to and fro, neither side being able to dislodge the other. But we had held our ground; and the greatest credit is due to General Auchinleck for having robbed Rommel of the fruits of his victory by this successful stand after so long a retreat.

During the following month, two considerable attacks by our forces improved our positions, but showed that the enemy was too strongly consolidated to be shifted by anything short of a large-scale offensive. But the door was shut tight against anything less on his part also. General Auchinleck was succeeded as C.-in-C. Middle East by General Alexander, who had been the last man to leave Dunkirk and had so brilliantly brought our small army safely out of Burma. General Montgomery succeeded General Ritchie in command of the Eighth Army.

These changes had hardly taken effect when Rommel made a serious bid to break through.

Our lines to the south, towards the Qattara Depression, had been (probably deliberately) left gappy. If the enemy had tried a headlong rush through, he could have been met by a heavy blow from the north against his flank and by a reserve army moving out from the Delta in his front.

On August 30th, in a night attack, the enemy did break through this lightly defended southern sector between the Ruweisat ridge and Himeimat, and having blocked the southern edge of this gap, he turned north behind our lines and made for the coast with the intention of bringing our armour to battle. The bait was refused. Remaining on the defensive, the Eighth Army, during three days, hit back at the enemy with bombing, artillery fire, and concentric harassing attacks. He dared not leave an unbroken army on his flank; supplies were difficult to come by and petrol was running short. On September 3rd, having been badly mauled, he began to retire. Under cover of three fierce attacks next day, he hauled his men and armour off, with nothing to show for heavy losses except the occupation of the original no-man's land on the southern sector.

We did not follow up this repulse, though it was a substantial defensive victory, for six

GENERAL SIR HAROLD ALEXANDER, COMMANDER-IN-CHIEF, MIDDLE EAST.

weeks. There were sound reasons for this caution. General Alexander wanted to make sure that once he started he could go on. He was still training the 10th Corps—designed as the spear-head of his armour—far behind the front; and all the time more and more essential material was arriving in Egypt.

For the victory which this book portrays was not suddenly improvised. In his preliminary review of the battle which started on October 23rd, the Prime Minister showed how victory was built up by long-term planning. The United Kingdom divisions (the 44th, 50th and 51st) which gave new weight to our assault, actually left these islands in May and June. When the news of the fall of Tobruk reached the Prime Minister, he was in the United States consulting President Roosevelt. The President at once ordered the despatch of the first batch of Sherman tanks to the Middle East, even withdrawing from the U.S. Army many of those already delivered. A few hundred more of the British six-pounder anti-tank guns would probably have saved us from defeat at Gazala. They were there in quantity at El Alamein, and the tremendous value of the American supplies should not obscure the fact, which President Roosevelt so generously made public, that all but a fraction of the Eighth Army's equipment came from British factories. The scale of air reinforcement is shown in the use of no fewer than seven hundred bombers in the attack, which virtually grounded and disrupted the enemy's air force.

These preparations were, however, only in line with the consistent determination of the United Kingdom Government to hold and then to extend the bastion of the Middle East. More remarkable even than the torrent of reinforcements which poured into Egypt between May and November, 1942, was the steady trickle which reached there even at the time of Dunkirk when there was not one fully-equipped division in these islands to resist imminent invasion. In times of scarcity as in times of abundance the Middle East fronts were first patched and then galvanised. Something new was always going into Africa.

A word should be added about the photographers who took almost all the pictures in this book. They belong to No. 1 Army Film and Photo Section, attached to the Public Relations Service in the Middle East. It is hoped that the reader may feel inclined to agree that the lens, if not mightier than the sword, has done the sword full justice.

SUEZ, SEPTEMBER 1942

The great offensive is being prepared. Newly arrived from Britain, infantry of the Highland Division complete their training in desert marches.

Sand whirls from the face of the desert as the artillerymen fire the 25-pounder guns. which were the main instrument of the great barrage.

Sappers practise their dangerous and intricate task. The leader holds the mine detector, the second man places a marker over each located mine.

Officers of the armoured divisions cluster on the welded frame of a Sherman tank, examining the turret and 360-degree traverse 75 mm. gun.

I. THE LONG MONTHS OF PREPARATION

The British Eighth Army trained and fought at the end of the longest supply line of any Allied fighting force anywhere in the world. The four and five months' journey that brought Highlanders and Home Counties men, Shermans and Crusaders, 25-pounders and anti-tank guns and mine detectors to the Middle East bastion of Allied power stretched 12,000 miles. At least a quarter of the route was exposed to the danger of submarine and air attack. The Axis supply line across the Mediterranean was short. Much Axis material was sunk : but much got through. The Axis command believed its own stories of sinkings. It disbelieved the Allies' stories about building. Rommel calculated that he was bound to win the race of supply and reinforcement. On October 3rd, twenty days before the Eighth Army attacked, he said in Berlin: " We hold the Gateway of Egypt with the full intention to act. We did not go there with any intention of being flung back sooner or later. You may rely on our holding fast to what we have got." They were Famous Last Words.

WELL TRAINED NOW, AND ACCUSTOMED TO THEIR NEW WEAPONS, THE TANK CREWS CLAMBER INTO A LINE OF SHERMANS. THE HOUR OF ATTACK IS NEAR.

OVER THESE MOONLIT SANDS THE INFANTRY WILL COME. THE GUNS ARE GLOWING IN THE DISTANCE. THE CAMERAMAN WAS A MILE FROM THE ENEMY.

SPACED ONE TO EVERY TWENTY-THREE YARDS, THE GUNS OF THE EIGHTH ARMY THUNDER OUT IN THE HEAVIEST BARRAGE THE WESTERN DESERT HAS KNOWN.

II. THE HOUR OF ATTACK

The Battle of Egypt began at precisely 9.30 p.m. on Friday, October 23rd. On a front of over six miles one British gun every 23 yards poured a tornado of fire upon the deep zone of enemy defences. The barrage raged at its height for 20 minutes. A night of brilliant moonlight was chosen. When their turn came, the infantry would be able to see. This sector of six miles was in the north of the forty-mile line between El Alamein and the Qattara Depression. Both the form of the attack and the sector chosen were a surprise to the enemy. For the sector chosen was that which the enemy held most strongly. Here he had concentrated most of his two German infantry divisions, one German Panzer division, one Italian armoured division, and two Italian motorised divisions. If, as he expected, the Eighth Army attacked in the centre, then this powerful force was to be flung into an over-whelming flank counter-attack. The trap was refused. The Eighth Army attacked in the north where the enemy could meet its advance only by frontal counter-attack. The form of attack—blasting a gap for infantry by short hurricane bombardment—went back to 1916-18. It had fallen into disrepute, because casualties were heavy and against an easily reinforceable line the advance could rarely go far or fast enough for a break through. But in Egypt the going was not Passchendaele mud, and Rommel's line, in the short run, was not easily reinforceable. Nearly everything he had was already in it. The hammering of 1916 forced the enemy back to the Hindenburg line in the spring of 1917. What happened then in nine months happened now in as many days; and Rommel's nearest Hindenburg line was 700 miles away.

25-pounder gun crews bend to their task.

7

III. THE INFANTRY BREAKS THROUGH

At 10 p.m. on October 23rd the United Kingdom and Dominion infantry advanced. By 5.30 a.m. next morning they were on a line six miles long, four miles west of the enemy's advanced minefields. It was their task during the next days to widen and deepen this first salient until its nose was out on the other side of the enemy's minefields and defences, and a clear road for the tanks had been won; to convert break-in to break-through. For the moment further minefields to the west pre-vented any general advance. October 25th passed in relative quiet, but that night Australians on the north and Highlanders on the south widened the salient. During the next six days—until November 1st—all the enemy counter-attacks were met and broken by Eighth Army guns and infantry. Night after night the advance made gradual progress. The men who did this job belonged to these Divisions—the 44th; the 50th; the 51st Highland, with the bitter day of St. Valery to avenge; the 2nd New Zealand (the "ball of fire"); the 9th Australian; the 1st South African; the 4th Indian, veterans of Keren; and contingents of Greeks and Fighting French. They inflicted casualties of five to one on the pick of Axis troops. Then on the night of November 1st-2nd, a Brigade each from the 50th and 51st Divisions and the New Zealanders, on a front of four miles, pushed the nose of the salient three miles further west. It was the break-through.

Through the dust and smoke of enemy shell fire the infantry leap forward for the advance, making first for the enemy strong-points that bar their way.

Nearing the enemy, the leader of these Australians crouches, revolver in one hand, steadying himself on the rocky outcrop with the other.

The strong-point is overrun. The trampled field telephone wires on the desert sand lead to the wrecked gun, beside which a German soldier lies dead.

The first German prisoners are brought in from the overrun strong-points. Soon they will be on their way towards the rear and the prisoner camps.

The advance goes on. Two men of a Home Counties regiment are setting their Vickers gun on the soft sand as an enemy shell bursts ahead of them.

As these men take cover behind a knocked-out enemy tank, a shell bursts close to the other side of it. Then on they go to their next objective.

INFANTRYMAN, EGYPT 1942

THE ADVANCE WIDENS OUT AFTER THE FIRST STRONG-POINTS ARE OVERRUN.   IN OPEN FORMATION. NOW CROUCHING. NOW RUNNING. TH

IN AN AREA CLEARED BY THE INFANTRY, LORRIES, TRUCKS AND CARS GATHER IN A SCATTERED CIRCLE, ABOUT TO MOVE FURTHER UP.

INFANTRY MOVE FORWARD. ON THE OPEN DESERT, EACH IS A TARGET. LEADING MEN ARE CLOSING IN TO TAKE A PRISONER, ARMS RAISED.

BELOW, THE ENEMY, FIERCELY BUT VAINLY CONTESTING THE ADVANCE, LAUNCHES A STUKA RAID ON EIGHTH ARMY TRANSPORT

TWENTY-ONE BOMBS GO CRASHING DOWN ON ENEMY POSITIONS FROM A FORMATION OF BOMBERS OF THE ALLIED AIR FORCES. THEY ARE MITCHELL B25's.

IV. AIR FORCE AND ARMY FIGHT AS ONE

Co-operation between army and air force was perfected in the Battle of Egypt. There was no question of divided command, said General Montgomery. There was only one command. During the whole of the land lull between Rommel's defeat in the first week of September and the attack on October 23rd, the Allied Air Forces pounded the enemy's back areas and supply lines. With the British submarines, they ensured that not a tanker got through. Four-fifths of all the ships that sailed in this period from Italian or Greek ports were sunk or damaged. The Axis air force was swept from the skies. On October 23rd a terrific attack, involving well over a thousand sorties by bombers and fighters, was made on enemy airfields, lines of communication, and .concentrations of guns and troops in and behind his lines. Two facts show what this attack meant to the Eighth Army. Its advancing troops were rarely attacked from the air; and 550 Axis aircraft, destroyed or grounded for lack of fuel, were found on the enemy's airfields when they were captured. During the advance, the Allied air forces helped to frustrate many counter-attacks.

Enemy transport is bombed hour after hour.

Petrol bowsers burn fiercely after an air attack.

British and American aircraft raid Fuka airfield.

It is night-time when the sappers start their work.

One by one every mine between the tapes is found.

The sand scooped away, the igniter is removed

V. CLEARING THE GAP FOR THE ARMOUR

The enemy's line of defence at El Alamein consisted of great patches of mines with strong machine-gun points in the gaps between them. The ground won by the infantry had to be cleared of mines by the sappers before it was safe for the armour. Mines are to tanks what barbed wire is to infantry. They are buried just below the sand surface in staggered groups. They are detected with an electrical instrument like a vacuum cleaner. The Eighth Army's sappers were busy every night for two weeks before the advance, sweeping them up. All through the first nine days of the battle they went on with their delicate and dangerous job. The technique of laying minefields has been highly developed. They must be marked in some way so that the forces they are meant to defend do not themselves run into them. The most usual way is to surround the fields with a strand or two of barbed wire. It is therefore easy to pretend there are minefields where, in fact, there are none by running up such enclosures. The enemy will at least have to test them for mines before he dares to advance. The sappers successfully and swiftly overcame the obstacles of real and dud booby traps, so opening the road for the armour.

The mine is eased from its shallow bed in the sand.

Gently and carefully, the sapper puts it aside,

THE GAP IS CLEAR FOR THE TANKS. THE SIGNPOST IS HAMMERED IN, WHITE POINT TOWARDS THE GAP, RED TAIL TOWARDS THE UNCLEARED FIELD.

GENERAL MONTGOMERY WATCHES HIS TANKS MOVE UP

VI. THE TANKS GO UP TO BATTLE

PENNANTS PROUDLY FLYING, A LONG LINE OF CRUSADER TANKS SWEEPS FORWARD TO MEET THE PANZER DIVISIONS.

By early morning on November 2nd the infantry and sappers had done their work. The tanks went up to bring the enemy tanks to battle. During the June-July battles the Eighth Army had suffered, amongst other things, from a shortage of heavy tanks. In October there was no longer any such handicap. There were the Crusaders from Britain, and from America the Grants and Shermans. These last were to prove a full match for the Germans' heaviest armour. The crews of the Armoured Divisions were almost exclusively United Kingdom troops, including most of the famous cavalry and yeomanry regiments and men of the Royal Tank Regiment. Until November 2nd there had been only minor tank engagements, though

some of the British tanks followed the infantry in their first advance. The British armour was still practically intact; the enemy had suffered severely in abortive counter-attacks. This favourable balance had been secured not only by new British tactics, but also by complete tactical surprise. The Tenth Corps, consisting of two armoured divisions and the New Zealand infantry division, was encamped for training in the Delta, far behind the battle front. As far as enemy air reconnaissance could detect, it was still there on October 22nd, the day before the attack. But it was not there. The whole corps, leaving behind a dummy camp, had been moved up to the line. All day long on November 2nd the great tank battle raged at El Aqqaqir. It wast the turning point.

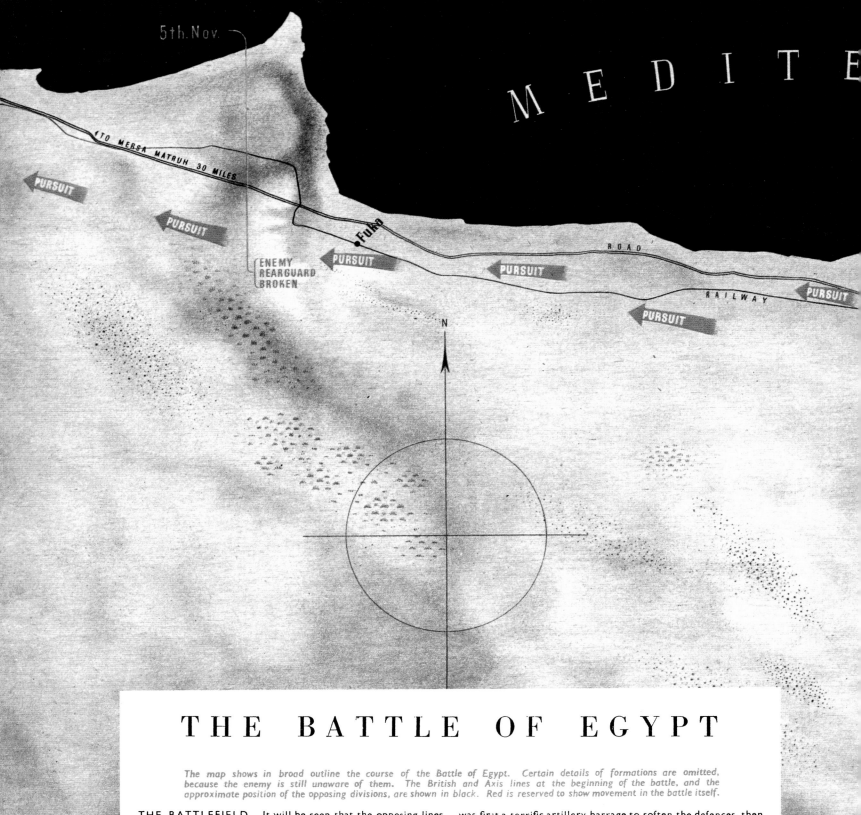

5th. Nov.

‹TO MERSA MATRUH 30 MILES

PURSUIT

PURSUIT

Fuka

ENEMY
REARGUARD
BROKEN

PURSUIT

PURSUIT

PURSUIT

PURSUIT

ROAD

RAILWAY

PURSUIT

M E D I T E

N

THE BATTLE OF EGYPT

The map shows in broad outline the course of the Battle of Egypt. Certain details of formations are omitted, because the enemy is still unaware of them. The British and Axis lines at the beginning of the battle, and the approximate position of the opposing divisions, are shown in black. Red is reserved to show movement in the battle itself.

THE BATTLEFIELD. It will be seen that the opposing lines on October 23rd, the eve of battle, stretched for forty miles from the sea to the cliffs of the impassable Qattara Depression. In the south of the line the desert is broken by rocky outcrops. In the centre there are ridges and hillocks where sand covers the underlying rock. In the north it is sandier and flatter, and the road and railway run over level ground just south of the salt marshes that fringe the sea. The British and enemy lines consisted of discontinuous belts of minefields interspersed with strong-points and machine-gun and anti-tank gun emplacements.

THE ORDER OF BATTLE. The map shows that Rommel had divided his armour half-and-half between north and south. The greater part of the German infantry were in the north. The Italian infantry were mainly in the south, where they were stiffened by some Germans. The centre was weakly held by Italian infantry. The Eighth Army was more evenly spread. The Tenth Corps, the striking force which was later to exploit the break-through, was waiting fifty miles to the east.

THE TACTICS. Rommel probably expected the Eighth Army to attack in the centre, from the Ruweisat ridge, and against that part of his line least strongly held. Had it done so, he would have tried to crush it between his Panzer Divisions converging from north and south. But it did not. The Eighth Army attacked not the weakest but the strongest part of Rommel's line, the north. The method of attack, in sequence,

was first a terrific artillery barrage to soften the defences, then the driving by the infantry of a wedge right through the enemy's lines, and then the final stroke by the armour. That was what was tactically planned. That was what actually happened.

THE COURSE OF THE BATTLE. The Battle of Egypt can be divided into three phases, all shown on the map. **(a) The infantry advance and break-through** in the north, October 23rd—November 1st-2nd. The three red lines show the stages reached by this infantry advance on three dates— October 24th, after one night's fighting ; October 27th, after another three days ; November 1st-2nd, the night of the break-through. **(b) The tank battle at El Aqqaqir,** November 2nd. to which the road had been opened by the infantry advance. **(c) The pursuit,** November 3rd— November 11th-12th, when Egypt was cleared of the enemy. The Battle of Egypt was therefore decided in the north, where tank battle followed break-through and pursuit followed tank battle. Here the fighting was always bitter and heavy, pure Blitzkrieg. In the centre and south, as the map shows, the fighting was secondary and shaped by events in the north. The diversionary attack in the south was called off as soon as its purpose was served. The map also makes it clear that the effect of the break-through was to divide the Axis army into two sections, between which contact was lost. From the north infantry swung across the only possible line of retreat of the Italians in the south, and they were rounded up in thousands.

Q a t t a r a   D e p r e

MILES 0   10   20

RANEAN SEA

5th. Nov.

3rd. Nov.

Break through
1st. Nov.

2nd. Advance
27th. Oct.

1st. Advance
24th. Oct.

El Daba

AXIS
AIRFIELDS
OCCUPIED

PURSUIT

Sidi Abd
El Rahman

ENEMY TANKS

GERMAN FORCE HOLDS OUT
TILL 3rd. NOV.

FULL
ENEMY
RETREAT
BEGINS

**15th.
PANZER**

LITTORIO
(ARMOURED)

164th.

Thompson's
Post

PURSUIT

TRIESTE

ENEMY DEFENCES

AUST.

AREA
OF TANK
BATTLE
2nd. NOV.

N.Z. & 51st.

90th.
LIGHT

Tell El
Eisa

**9th.
AUST-
RALIAN**

Kidney
Ridge

ROAD

RAILWAY

51st. & 50th.

U.K. ARMOURED CORPS GOES THROUGH C...

N.Z. SWING
SOUTH TO CUT
OFF ITALIANS
3rd. NOV.

Tell El
Aqqaqir

El Alamein

ENEMY TANK
CONCENTRATION
BOMBED BY
R.A.F. 28th. OCT.

FOLLOWED BY
ARMOURED DIV.
FROM SOUTH

N.Z.

**1st.
STH.
AFRI-
CAN**

TO ALEXANDRIA, 45 MILES

2nd. NEW ZEALAND DIVISION
IN RESERVE FURTHER EAST

S.A. PATROLS
RAIDING IN REAR
OF ITALIANS
5th. NOV.

Ruweisat Ridge

TWO U.K. ARMOURED DIVs.
50 MILES FURTHER EAST

10th. CORPS

BOLOGNA

AXIS TANKS MOVE NORTH TO MEET 1st. BRITISH ATTACK

MAIN ENEMY DEFENCES (MINES & STRONG-POINTS)

4th.

**4th.
INDIAN**

MOVES TO NORTH
BEFORE BATTLE

**51st.
HIGH-
LAND**

**21st.
PANZER**

**ARIETE
(ARMOURED)**

ONE U.K. BRIGADE NORTH TO SALIENT 29th. Oct.

BRITISH DEFENCES (MINES & STRONG-POINTS)

**44th.
(TACTICAL
RESERVE)**

**GERMAN
INFANTRY**

BRESCIA

50th.

**50th.
INCLUDING
FIGHTING
FRENCH
& GREEKS**

ALL ARMOUR TO NORTH 3rd. NOV.

**GERMAN
INFANTRY**

FORWARD ENEMY DEFENCES

FULGORE

Deir El
Munassib

44th.

ITALIANS BEGIN
TO SURRENDER

PAVIA

MINEFIELDS
CLEARED 24th. OCT.

Himeimat

FULL
ENEMY
RETREAT
BEGINS

**GERMAN
INFANTRY**

**U.K.
ARMOURED
DIVISION**

DIVERSIONARY ATTACK
DISCONTINUED 25th. OCT.

...sion

2nd. Nov.

6th. Nov.

...Oct.

50

The tank crews of the Armoured Divisions make their last preparations for the impending battle. A Crusader gets part of her fill of petrol

THIRTY TONS OF STREAMLINED STEEL, THE SHERMANS MOVE OFF TO THE BATTLE.   THE INFANTRY HAS BROKEN THROUGH, AND IS HOLDING THE W

With the dust from the tank-beaten track swirling around them, the crew of a General Grant ride up towards the battlefield.

...st behind the line a tank is loaded with ammunition.

Big shells are stacked in for the Sherman's 75 mm. gun.

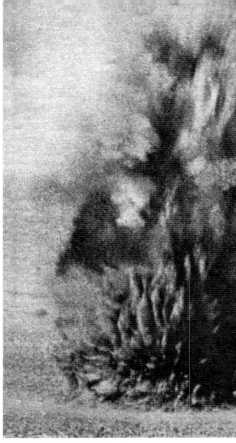

The battle bursts.   Unscathed, a Crusader races through the smoke of a heavy enemy bomb.

Swerving violently, another British tank speed

It is the height of battle.   Knocked out German tanks begin to litter the desert.

As the day passes, more and more enemy tan

Anti-tank gunners are in the battle, engaging the enemy armour, protecting their own.

The shells have been fired, the battle is won.

ar miss.

First blood: a German Mark III special tank lies furiously ablaze after a direct hit early in the battle.

led and silenced.

In clouds of dust raised by the blast of their own guns, a force of twenty British tanks pound the enemy.

rman is restocked with ammunition.

Throughout the battle, tank recovery men have kept the British armour at strength.   Their rest is earned.

21

VII. DEATH OF THE PANZERS AT

In the Battle of Egypt there were two decisive events. The first was the infantry break-through. The second was the great tank battle at El Aqqaqir. The first made the second possible. The second sealed the success of the first. The first was completed in just over nine days. The second was over in about as many hours.

When it was over, El Aqqaqir was a cemetery of Axis armour, and the Battle of Egypt was in fact won. The rest was pursuit. The tank battle was fought on November 2. By November 1 the enemy had been compelled to mass virtually all his armour in the area to the west of Kidney Ridge, where the main Eighth Army

EL AQQAQIR

infantry advance had been made and from which the break-through was threatened. By this time the Eighth Army had inflicted on the enemy armour losses out of all proportion to the magnitude of the relatively minor tank engagements which had been fought ; and by forcing him to mass his armour in one force in the north

they had made frontal attack his only form of counter action, instead of the double flank attack he had planned. A few hours after the infantry break-through on the night of November 1–2, and before daylight, an armoured regiment was raiding far behind the enemy's lines, and an armoured division and another armoured brigade was pressing westwards. Through the hours of daylight the tank battle of El Aqqaqir raged violently, with heavy losses on both sides. The enemy was broken, and on the night of November 2–3 El Aqqaqir was captured. The Eighth Army communique of November 5 said that two hundred and sixty German and Italian tanks had so far been counted as destroyed.

The crumpled track of a German Mark IV tank.

Gun and superstructure are blown wildly vertical.

The mangled ruins of a Mark III.

THIS IS THE GRAVEYARD OF GERMAN TANKS. FIRE LICKS THE HULK OF A MARK

Looking like a doomed ship, this crippled enemy tank is blown up by British engineers.

Torn steel of a Mark IV.

BATTLEFIELD OF EL AQQAQIR. THE BATTLE HAS PASSED ON. IT IS NOW A PURSUIT.

Smashed and burnt out, its **gun** barrel snapped.

25

DESERTED AND DEPRIVED OF THEIR TRANSPORT BY THE GERMANS, AND CUT OFF BY NEW ZEALANDERS, DROVES OF ITALIAN PRISONERS ARE ROUNDED U

VIII. THE BROKEN ARMIES

The pitched battle of October 23rd–November 2nd broke the enem armies. On November 2nd, the day of the tank battle, there we already signs of infantry withdrawal all along the front. O November 3rd these signs became very definite. In the south, th Italian divisions could not retreat far, for they were abandone by the Germans, who commandeered all transport for their ow men. Hardly a man of the six Italian infantry divisions escapec Droves of prisoners were taken. The German 164th infantr division also practically ceased to exist. Even though the Germar were first to retreat after the battle was lost, they left behind ov 8,000 prisoners, apart from their killed and wounded. Among th Germans captured were General Ritter von Thoma, commande of the Afrika Korps, and Major Burckhardt, commander of th German paratroops. Among the Italians captured were th commanders of the Pavia and Trento divisions. The Battle c Egypt cost the Axis 75,000 men, over 500 tanks and over 1,000 guns

The march to Alexandria.

German prisoners wait to be taken to the back areas.

OUTFOUGHT IN THEIR OWN ART OF SWIFT ARMOURED WARFARE, AND CAPTURED BY HIGHLANDERS, THESE GERMANS, WITH 8,000 MORE, PASS TO PRISON CAMPS.

VON THOMA
Commander, Afrika Korps

MASINA
Commander, Trento Division

BIGNAMI
General, Folgore Division

BURCKHARDT
German paratroop leader

BRUNETTI
Commander, Brescia Division

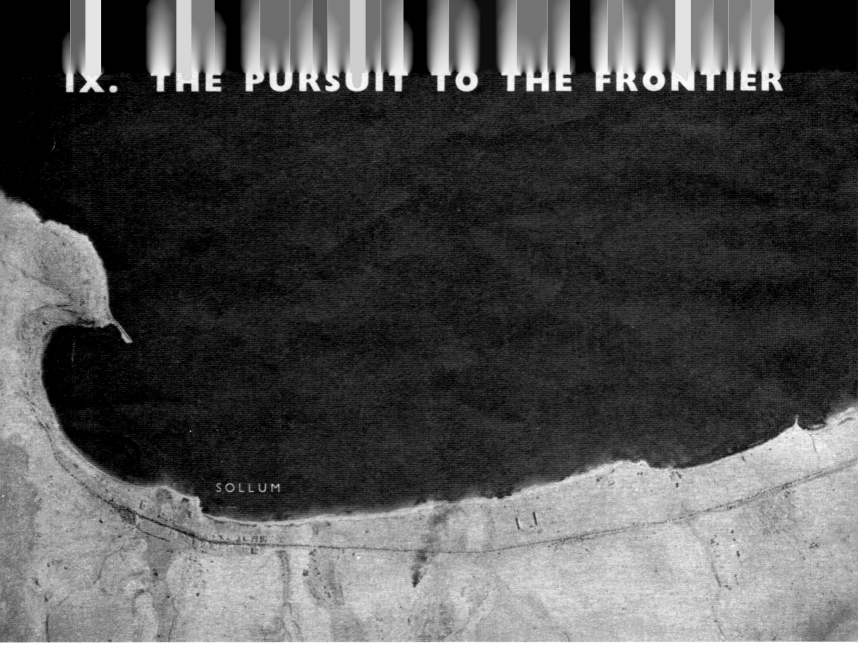

THIS REMARKABLE PHOTOGRAPH SHOWS ENEMY VEHICLES STREAMING WEST ALONG THE COAST ROAD TO SOLLUM, LAST POINT IN EGYPT. TRAFFIC IS ASC

WITH the tank battle won, the pursuit began. On November 4th the world heard officially from the Middle East communique that the enemy was " in full retreat." It was to take less than eight days of thunderous pursuit to clear him out of Egypt. In the north he maintained for some days a gradually thinning screen of tanks and anti-tank guns. He tried to make some sort of first stand on the Fuka escarpment, but this was broken on November 6th, his rearguard cut off by the British armour, and his remnants pursued further to the west. The pursuit was severely hampered by terrific rains, but on November 8th the ground dried a little and the British armour reached a point south of Mersa Matruh, while the motorised infantry were approaching Sidi Barrani. On November 10th another rearguard was broken at Buq-Buq. The next day Halfaya and Sollum were captured. On November 12th the whole frontier area was cleared. The enemy was out of Egypt. Meanwhile, in the south the abandoned Italians wandering in the desert were rounded up. Enemy losses during the pursuit were heavy. The advancing Eighth Army found the roads and tracks littered w lorries and equipment destroyed in the cea less air attacks. Distance did not save enemy, for the Allied Air Forces bound forward to operate from captured airfiel We leave the story at the frontier, w thousands of prisoners trudging east and remains of the Axis army flying west und a rain of fire to pick up what streng they could from reserves in Cyrenaica a Tripolitania. It was the first stage in victory which has already brought the Eigh Army to the approaches to Tripoli.

THIS ENLARGEMENT SHOWS THE GREAT TRAFFIC JAM IN SOLLUM. VEHICLES ON THE ROAD ARE IN DOUBLE AND TREBLE LINES, BONNET TO TAILBOA

HALFAYA PASS

...A PASS (SHOWN TOP RIGHT) TO THE ALTERNATIVE ROUTE OF ESCAPE ALONG THE ESCARPMENT. THE WHOLE AREA IS PITTED WITH BOMB CRATERS

...e enemy left behind pockets of resistance and maintained a rear-...ard. These Shermans are beating down an isolated strongpoint.

The coast road was shelled in a vain effort to check the Eighth Army's advance. In the foreground is an abandoned enemy vehicle.

...LVOS OF BOMBS RAIN DOWN FROM ALLIED AIRCRAFT ON THE ENEMY VEHICLES RETREATING ALONG THE COAST ROAD BETWEEN EL DABA AND FUKA

Symbol of enemy resistance overcome, this 88 mm. gun was abandoned west of El Alamein.

Over 1,000 guns were captured in the battle and pursuit, including this 88 mm. in its emplacement.

The enemy was trying to haul this gun to safe when tractor and gun were wrecked by a direct h

Speed and power were the keynotes of the Eighth Army's advance along the coastal road. These Crusaders are racing after the retreating enemy. Their swiftness was especially valuable in the pursuit.

As the Eighth Army transport moved forward a in constant protective patrol. The lorr

El Daba airfield, littered with wrecked enemy aircraft, was occupied on November 5th the day after the full retreat began, by the R.A.F. Regiment.

Through hindering heavy rains, pursuing General Grants plough along past Fuka, where on November 6th an enemy rearguard was broken.

New Zealand forces advance along the now dry road towards Sidi Barrani on November 8th. The British armour was already near Mersa Matruh.

The Navy keeps the army supplied with water. A million and a half gallons are unloaded at Sollum, captured on November 11th.

ile gun, mounted on a tank chassis and
o the sand, found abandoned by the road.

Captured intact, this 150 mm. self-propelling heavy
German gun is being examined by British officers.

The enemy made no attempt to destroy or
salvage this crashed, slightly injured, Stuka.

st road, R.A.F. fighters raced overhead
R.A.F. supplies to new forward airfields.

British transport is bunched together in a dense stream on the coastal road. Faultless air cover has
made dispersal unnecessary   Normally, bunching like this would be asking for attack by enemy aircraft.

ALAMEIN TO EL AGHEILA, 750 MILES, THREE WEEKS.
Crusaders and Shermans pass through Mersa Matruh.

"The bright gleam has caught the helmets of our soldiers and warmed and cheered all our hearts."
WINSTON CHURCHILL, November 10th, 1942.